Collected Poems
of
CURTIS WETZEL

D1745362

Collected Poems

of

CURTIS WETZEL

CURTIS R. WETZEL

Library of Congress Control Number:		2015901110
ISBN:	Hardcover	978-1-5035-2766-9
	Softcover	978-1-5035-2767-6
	eBook	978-1-5035-2768-3

Print information available on the last page.

Rev. date: 02/24/2015

To order additional copies of this book, contact:
Xlibris
1-888-795-4274
www.Xlibris.com
Orders@Xlibris.com
702263

Contents

I dedicate this book to all of you.
I hope that my poems will enrich your life.
I Love You All.

Foreword

The poems for this book are from an accumulation of thoughts over a period of thirty-six years.

The poems that I have created are from personal experiences, or evolved from words, phrases, studies, or imagination, but all represent my thoughts. Thoughts from a poet who takes the pathless path, hence comes to different conclusions than we ordinarily do, for not being limited or bound to any conclusions or assumptions.

I enjoy the martial arts, which teach us the art of the living, all about ourselves, inside and out, and freedom.

I have enjoyed the wisdom from the old sages the most. The sage taught in the grove, and the sage learned and taught from all that nature has to offer. I have also enjoyed Taoism, Zen, and the Mystic, to name a few. The philosophical poems that I have written are from my own interpretations in a variety of forms.

I write with a wide variety of topics in my own way, nature, horticulture, solitude, philosophy, memories, and self-help. Ideas often begin on those all night missions. Some were, completely created. Some were, created with writing and rewriting by night and day enjoyment at home.

This selection has been, submitted for you by the urging of my heart. It is my hope that you will enjoy them as much as I do; it is also my hope that every time you read a poem, you will find new discoveries, in the same poem.

I'm The Mmg

I'm the MMG,
From the cosmos above;
Clay from the mountains
And from heart my love.

I'm in the garden,
I'm hidden within;
Formed from the dirt,
In which I am in.

I'm the MMG
I am and am not;
I'll reach for the treasure,
Then give it a shot.

I'm in the garden,
Sowing the seeds,
Working the soil
And maintaining its needs!

Welcome

I welcome you like spring,
That brings a new year.
Good tidings I bring
And I'm glad you are here.

You are welcome like the rain,
That brings forth life.
You are welcome from my heart,
That's been here from the start.

Take all the treasures
That your mind will hold;
Plant them to use,
Then behold.

Let go the frustration n' sorrow,
I bring you joy.
A new tomorrow,
Free to live and employ.

Take what is useful,
Let it go.
When it is useful,
It will be there to know.

Grow With Me

Come, grow with me and be my clone,
And we together but separate
Can have our own;
The fence rows, ditch banks, and beside the fields,
Where there's proper moisture for the yields.

And we together but separate meeting on the rocks,
Seeing our list to feed our flocks;
We mark an x to those that fall,
We're never discouraged,
Some are big and tall.

And we together but separate can walk thru the night,
Looking at the same stars our guidance and our light.
Holding guts of courage, our hoe, and our know;
The time for the next,
Or they'll be slow to grow.

Through the meadow of the finest weeds,
To the place where we planted our handpicked seeds;
Through the pickers, burrs, and sometimes cold,
We'll weed them and feed them,
And one day they'll all be buckets of gold.

These thoughts move our mind,
But when we're one with nature,
We're one of a kind.
If you're like the Gardener, you're never really alone,
Come grow with me and be my clone.

Will

You must be determined,
To find the will;
Work real hard,
You'll have your fill.

Follow your intuition,
Belong to the way of no way;
Keep your attention,
There'll be your pay.

There is no venture
Without risk;
A place for adventure,
For which may be brisk.

Step by step,
Along the way,
Plant for them,
For which they'll stay.

Belong, be strong.
They're not yours, until they're yours;
In which you'll last
And last along.

The Way

Day by day,
Through the night;
Making my way,
With the starlight!

Mile by mile,
Takes a while,
When it's over,
There, a smile!

In the night, dark and vast,
Take it easy, not too fast;
Dogs bark, coons fight,
Sometimes, with all their might!

To the gig a plot to dig,
Someday, they'll be great and big.
They're not mine, until they're fine,
Be patient and give them time.

A leaf on the river, a feather in the air,
Work with Nature, she's already there.
Birth, growth, maturity, and decay,
Become one with Nature, for this is the way.

Where To Go

Plowing soil
And sowing seeds,
Looking for places
And their weeds.

In the open,
Hurts to be,
Leave them there,
You will see.

Here and there, high n' low,
Plant the best and let them grow.
Keep it simple grab the hoe,
Where to go; only you should know.

In the beginning, they're slow to grow,
Do what you know and then awe and woe.
To the plants with love and care;
Bend them wrong, they will not fare.

Find some antlers, leave them there,
Pick them up, Karma, beware.
Holes in garments from the ground,
But the buds so big and round.

Nature's Way

As one
I rested upon Nature's way.
Being against her
Is difficult,
In which didn't pay.

When I tried on my own,
My way didn't make it a single day;
When I joined Nature, in her way,
T'was all in her control,
I learned not to manipulate, here in her sway.

Midnight Marijuana Gardener Warning

Marijuana Smoke Increases The Risk Of
Attachment And Heart Laughter,
Even In Nonsmokers.

The Trail

On my way to make a way,
Through the wild and the pay;
Like the dew on the grass,
The trail I'll pass.

People make them,
The deer take them.
Stay away from the trail,
Or you'll surely fail.

Follow the path
That has no trail;
Pick up the feet
And watch the tail.

To make a lane
Is to be followed by pain;
Cover your tracks,
Then you'll remain.

The Ride Home

My O my you've come so far.
Don't get caught, or you'll be a star.
So keep it straight, the car,
Or there'll be a scar.

You've got the whole world
In your hands;
So be careful,
Or they'll be in bands.

Buds a bouncing
In the back;
Keep, it going,
Don't look back.

Miles gone, miles to go,
Keep, it going, not too slow,
Don't glow, you'll show,
Then you'll need a tow.

Harvest

Under the old disturbed oak tree, able to see;
Reeking buds, sticky scissors, traumatized with glee.
Alongside delight, baskets, buzzes, and bees,
Amid treasure, for bowls, bongs, and blunts to be.

Cool brisk breezes blowing,
Buds and birds over head flowing.
Reaping, ready, ripened, and glowing,
There, in the wide-open, showing.

Yellow, orange, and brown leaves falling,
Purple, pink, and rose buds, calling;
Beautiful buds, standing bright,
In the sun, they're out of sight.

A little sorrow, losses, and pain,
Sometimes, through the pouring rain;
Holy smokes, over there look!
Those ones remain.

From the Gardener's gardens,
Glitzy golden walls,
Where towers with pearls and gems around,
I wish you all well, all around from pound to pound.

Truth

Truth is like a tree,
There in a field to see.
Always changing and free,
Like the leaves to be.

Truth has no shape, or form,
Like the clouds in the sky,
Forming and then reforming,
Alive, to move on by!

Truth is the true state of Nature.
Truth is like a thing you see.
Truth is like lightning, bright and fast,
And then gone in a flash, out of sight and past!

Truth is like water,
Fluid and graceful,
And the truth is like ice,
For which conforms to fact.

Here And Now

Here and now, not the past or future.
There is neither past nor future,
But the living now,
And now is the time for the how.

Fear leads us to cling,
From discovery through learning
With no conclusions,
The freedom to fling!

To know and understand yourself,
Is to know and understand everyone else.
Not trying to be like anyone else,
But to be purely yourself.

To live is to learn,
To learn is to live.
To be perfect,
Is to invite not being perfect.

Like the cocoon for the butterfly,
So is the body for the soul.
Like a stone after the chisel,
Thee attainments and toll.

Care

They're from me,
There in the soil, from my toil,
A plot for your fare, the tare;
Now for all I share the care and dare.

Plants come and spots go.
I give and gave my all, for you all,
Great and lo;
For this I'm called and know.

To nothing I'm attached like the breeze,
A desire less Spirit and free.
Not even freedom has a chain on me,
There in the whole, to be.

Seasons come and seasons go,
Like the grass and then the snow.
My time here is ending and slow,
This I recognize and show.

Hunting

It is a cold October morning,
The frost is on the ground.
Toward the East, the sun is forming,
There in the circumference, not a sound.

Perched in a tree stand,
With scissors in hand;
There around, is the new strand.
Add them up, there's definitely a grand.

The deer are there,
They're not safe, but sound;
They snort,
Because, I am found!

Looking at the glee,
That lets them go free.
They wander on by,
For they can see!

Patience

It's October, the time for fun,
Some buds are still forming; they're in the sun.
Leave them be, not all are done.
Don't pick them early, maybe one.

Remember!
It's October, the time for fun.
Salmon are in the river, for their run,
So cast a line, to catch maybe one.

Look, the geese are flying from the North,
They're in no hurry, they're back and forth.
The time for squirrels to gather nuts,
They'll be set for winter, in your guts.

From the South, a fox,
His paws are full
With prey in his mouth;
If it comes in close, then make a box.

If the plants are still green,
Leave them be;
Let them finish,
At least they're still seen.

Primal

The primal is not attached to anything here,
When attached, behold terrors and tears.
Utilizing every way,
For which motivation will pay.

Mastering the will,
For the great hill,
Or deep valley,
Or bright, or dark ally, or alley!

Nature's taking her own course,
For reality is the pathless path.
The way of life,
Where there is no strife.

Destroy the desires,
The instincts to preserve;
Guard the heart,
And clear the mind to its own true center.

The Noble War

The noble war
Is from within,
For our own frustrations and follies
That must be pinned.

Therein lies the battle,
For which one must win.
The blinding hates, angers, and bias
That Ego has one in.

The chains of illusion and delusion,
For which one must win.
Behold the spiritual power,
That's already within.

To overcome,
Is being where you begin;
Therein is the power to win,
All along there it has been.

Undivided And Unbound

There's a lot of suffering and needs,
For God already gave us the priceless seeds.
Beholding, God already gave us the tools;
And underneath all the blinding dirt,
Behold,
The gems and jewels!

If your heart is heavy and bound,
You,
Come from freedom and power,
Where you were once together and found;
The place where you can return, right now,
Safe and sound; undivided and unbound!

When you're walking off the trail,
Where, nothing leads you by the tale, or tail.
And when you find the heart,
Where, you will not fail.
The place undivided and unbound,
Where, you can walk as one to prevail.

And when you can be together as a whole,
Into the entire, with your heart and soul,
There! You'll be able to see,
Free and clear,
Undivided and unbound!

Good From Bad

When you are feeling sad and on your own,
And everything you touch crumbles that can't be sown;
The reasons are not obvious,
The unknown!
Just clear the mind, to gather the senses,
And keep in mind the center, to re-own.

Gathering treasures for the mortal,
In a world that teaches through experience.
Not for the mortal,
But for the immortal;
Through the laws of Nature,
And by ways of cause and effect.

The good comes from the bad,
Without the bad, there would be no good.
From everything that is bad, therein, behold the good.
God wouldn't have us divided, or ignorant,
In a place of chaos,
Here in the hood.

Garments And Virtues

Being mortal and immortal is like a book and mirror.
You can pick the book up and open it mortally,
But you can only grasp the content immortally.
We all have our own attainments book and image,
In which our image will be dressed
With our attainments and virtues.

Completeness

There is, no I, but one in all.
Where there is separation from the whole,
There is no completeness of the Soul,
But incompleteness and fear of the toll.

When we move, there is no I,
But a passion, for the I creates fashions
That argues with the naturalness
Of passion!

Where there is passion,
There is no time for distinction or fashion.
Where there is distinction and fashion,
There is separation from the whole, the Soul.

Daily Decrease

In the forest, there are many trees,
They are all the same, but different.
Many leaves fall to form a mature tree,
Many times trees fall for just trying to be.
Only when leaves are all finished fallen,
Is the tree unattached and free?

A Plant In The Field

A plant in the field that stands there alone,
Its bountiful increase will stand to be, shone.
Still we keep it quiet to sleep,
Full of sweet dreams and itchy eyes,
Still tomorrow, not even a peep.

With every day that passes by,
When we see her again, we look up to the sky.
A plant of beauty that glitters and sways,
Made for the wolves,
There are only so many days.

Tao

To be and not to be
Like stillness
In the motion of the sea
Merging
With the wind
Without effort, flexible, and free

All's For You

Grow to attain,
Let go to maintain.
There's treasure within that lives,
And for you, it loves and gives.
All is for you, are you ready?
Are you being real?
Or are you blinded by pessimism n' fancy?

Boundless Boundaries

It's ten pm; the sun is past the sphere;
The night has taken form, not all are silent yet but dark
And it is here.
Freedom of the night,
Where there are boundless boundaries to be and see.

I'm in the night, the place I love to be;
Passing the path, to, be boundless and free.
All in all and all in me;
Look up, look in,
The cosmos you see.

All is for me you see,
Passing the path, to, be boundless and free.
Along my journey to my favorite tree,
I stop for but a moment
And it, reminds me how not to be.

On I go with this I know,
There are no boundaries,
Except the one I sow.
A bug in the eye, in which gave its life,
To remind me how not to, see.

And low the owl;
It reminds me
That for all I know,
I know
Not!

Declaration Of Another Wall

If the kindness of a plant has the power,
To ease the sickness, oppressions, woes, and pain;
Let us reconsider for all the potential,
To explore, to remain!
To let the potential be an aid to all,
Not to seek disarray, or to destroy,
For therein are joy and the freedom from the fall,
To be unlimited, to advance, to employ!

Still we can always cancel to return,
So let us tomorrow hold the blessings intern,
To free the chains we placed on yesterday,
So that we can, return and renew for a better today.
Once through the mighty hall,
To the place of freedom
And liberation,
For tearing down another wall!

The Bud Bouquet

I sent you the bouquet to say,
I really like you and your way.
Just forget the attachments way,
To be happy and free every day.
When I seen you beautiful and bright,
There was laughter and sight.
I treated you as if you weren't mine,
In some way, I knew you were all fine.

Forget the troubles and foe,
Because, I'm over here for you to know.
Let go the past to walk along,
To be free where there is no right or wrong.
Let your entire bitter x be past,
And remember me, without a cold blast.
Nobody will compel you to rise,
Wishing one day, I could look into your beautiful eyes.

When there's sorrow, loneliness, and the fiasco,
Just remember me, and the bouquet, a bud,
A friend so warm and true,
Maybe one day we can together be new?
Let go the burdens and woe,
And all will be given you to sow.
Be the nut you are, you're one of a find;
Wishing for the day, where I can be hard and kind.

The Mysterious Garden

On my way to the garden at bay,
Into the inlet there's a certain spirit at play.
Testing my courage, it finds a way,
There I am, still working my pay.

Sounds of steps walking through no way,
Where the mortal can't, there's no way.
Here it comes again, slow and sure,
I yelled hey!

There it was at my side,
Then, no sound,
Nowhere around;
There I am, still working my pay.

Riding back,
The wind was in my face and strong,
In which I didn't belong;
There it was at my back, pushing me along.

Pushed into the wind,
All the way back,
The time was short,
A kind friend of sort!

In Plain Sight

Beside a shanty stood a plant,
Stillness along a narrow path almost paved.
Seen with green, purple, glittering crystals, full and clear,
Her dress was colorful and cool,
As fresh as Mother Earth, herself.
An occupant often stood at the shanty window leaning out,
Listening to the sounds Nature makes.
A sweet constant smell, still the same,
Although getting stronger, a lot stronger, as fall went on
She gathered weight from the fresh moist soil
To place within her buds; when the herb
Of summer dripped from the all day sun,
She stood next to the shanty window occupant,
Dreamily, listening to, Nature's songs!
Ripe were her buds, her stature smelled,
Natural beauty and naturally belongs.

O Holy Mother

O Holy Mother, how wild are thee,
That my mind must know?
A veiled unseen presence to be,
Like the ambiguity of snow.

O Holy Mother, remember me, I'm empty, cold, and low;
Love me and be in complete control.
I'm thine son formed to show;
Change my garments; make them fit for my soul.

Flee not like a leaf in the wind,
A wild spirit moving everywhere and nowhere;
My destroyer, my preserver, will you be kind?
To, hold and love me with your tender care.

O Holy Mother, remember me and show me your way,
Let not all, be a fancy dream,
Wherever I be or lay,
Flow through me as the stream.

Entreaty

The desire in heart
Speaks more clearly
Than all the fancy words of art.

The Lo Down Below

I stood over the bank in a hood
And watched the wolves go.
There in the middle, seeing
The, lo down below.

And over the hidden creek,
Over them every one,
Went the golden girls with a sneak,
All shined by the sun.

But when ringing rang inside,
And with girls of gold,
They're gone in a hurry,
Stumbling on, swift and bold!

My Pride

At sunset every day,
I stroll along an empty path and its way.
Along, like the wind I slide,
And it, which made me, is my pride.

Out amid the chaos and far,
Where doubt can place faith in a jar,
I fear neither the storm nor tide,
For it, which made me, is my pride.

Flesh n' bone,
Heart of stone;
From my pride,
Love n' light are shone.

Mighty Within

If you look inside and see things you don't like,
Be with it, therein, it'll take a hike.
If you've been and done things you regret,
Let go the past, don't fret.

When you wish you could be,
Just remember, you are, you see.
And when you feel weak, sad, and on your own,
Just remember who you are, go back, to-re-own.

When you're as low as low can be,
Look up! You see . . .
And when things are pulling you along,
A little push, you'll be strong.

Mighty is the spirit on the right,
To, hold on to, without a fight.
When the spirit on the left, starts a fight,
Give it your right, full of might.

Marijuana's Life

Beside the rivers, where the weeds are vigorous,
Where the best weeds rise;
The place where vegetation finds the vigorness,
To, grow up toward the skies.

Next to meadows, rivers, swamps, and swales,
Maybe a field way back;
Content, sometimes, drown,
A place for the golden crown.

Not knowing,
Life and death,
Stand the marijuana plants for their fates,
Along with other places for, their mates.

Plants not yet seen,
But strong and there;
Maybe with a male standing next to her keen,
To, preserve her sticky white hair.

Trembling; passing through the weeds to soar,
Through, doubt.
Where so many have failed before,
Choked out!

Foes somewhere, officers around,
Sought after, menaced, and betrayed;
No one there, none to help,
They just want them found.

The Surviving Blooms

Across the land,
Some may prey for the marijuana stand.
Let them go and remember the band,
There are others the same strand.

Planting where others fail,
Growing for blooms;
Along with other places,
Also being colorful blooms.

Over growing the vigorous weeds,
To, provide your needs.
Patiently waiting the lingering day,
Without a doubt, some will stay.

Remember the feet, to cross the path,
Not a single track for an eye.
Because assemblies
Meet and assemble, lo n' high.

Among the weeds, the place for seeds,
Little plants healthy with glee;
Not caring
What the assemblies and law might be?

To grow
Is all they know!
And like birds taking off,
Straight up and out they flow.

The Valuable Bud

In rich and fruitful soil,
Growing full of sun,
Buds on every branch,
Buds for everyone!

Sticky and sweet the valuable bud,
A natural beauty n' art;
They are
From Nature's huge heart!

So long they've grown to ease the pain,
And long they've found it hard to be;
Picked up and placed in a chain,
For being lonely and hurting, can't you see?

Never can you change Nature's fates,
But you can work around at will.
Just remember all the dates,
To weed, feed, and till.

Seasons Blessing

May the seasons fill the bucket of your heart?

That grows with the warmth of suns light.

And may that growth bring wealth to you,

Even if it's not right!

The Hoe

The handy hoe,
Beat up.
It's the only one
And gets dull to run.

In hand
Wherever I go,
If it lay there unhand
It could lay therein snow.

Dirty, old, handy hoe, seen lots of hikes,
Been to a lot of places,
Worked longer than lots of dirty, old, rusty bikes,
To till lots of spaces.

Harmony

Any passion or desire can result in loss of soul.
The pure spirit has no self, no merit, and no fame;
Being in union,
With the rhythm and forces in Nature.

A Day In The Night

Alone in the nighttime hours,
Resting on the ground;
Under a plant with many flowers,
Listening to, the wonder of sound.

Under the old silver moon
With brightness like that of high noon;
I rest unseen
Watchfully being keen.

Able to obtain
With no gain;
A way less way,
For which many are astray.

Beholding the skies,
Reflecting from hazel eyes;
For the night is still,
To wander, to till!

A venturous career
Where the nocturnal do appear;
Ecstasy no dreams,
Like roses n' streams.

Crossing Over

Crickets and frogs, the call to go,
There you are with guts n' hoe.
The night's young to wander far,
But in the sky, not even a star.
If a bad feeling passes you by,
And you don't know, looking up to the sky.
It's black n' dark,
And the dogs, not even a bark.
Should I go, or should I stay,
Maybe wait another day.
Tomorrow face it, face to face,
With such a list, there's definitely a place.
With one question, it's easy to sleep,
But the plants are in weeds way too deep.

The Seeds We Sow

Our words and choices grow like seeds.
Everything grows from seeds.
For every problem, there's a seed for the need.
Our words n' deeds are the soul made visible.
Positive words n' deeds are fruitful seeds.
Negative words n' deeds, like doubt n' hate, are weeds.

Positive seeds produce light and life.
Negative seeds produce darkness and strife.
We all have our own garden.
Our garden grows the seeds we sow.
If there's no love, plant seeds for love.
If there are weeds of doubt, plant seeds for faith.

If there are weeds of disappointment,
Plant seeds for encouragement.
And if there are weeds of sadness and loneliness,
Plant seeds for happiness and wholeness.
The seeds we sow burst forth to show,
So plant them in fertile soil and watch them grow.

Plant To Get

Places of gold,
Where buds produce many fold.
Over yonder, to and fro,
To the best; where the best yielders grow.
With you in mind,
Sweet buds many a kind.
Nature's not unfair,
Plant them back, they'll be for you there.

To conquer a place,
Plant for them in their face;
You'll find your efforts will pay.
The Gardener too advances everyday.
Adding plots in Gods earth,
Watching sprouts come forth a new birth.
Giving to all your very best,
Then Nature will finish, for you to rest.

The True Nature Of Mind

Superior virtue is not virtuous,
And here's virtue.
Never claim achievements.
Never act.
Nothing will be undone.
Act in accordance with things.
Leave no trace of self.
Perfect activity leaves no tracks.
Harmony never acts.
Harmony does everything.

No deliberate intervention or desire;
Deliberate intervention creates the opposite
Of what is intended, causing failure.
The primal, lives out of its original Nature,
Not tampered by knowledge,
Or restricted by mortality;
The undiminished vitality of the new born state,
Reverted to infancy; born again to pure spirit.
The ego robs an individual from totality.
The learned have returned to the pure primal, simplicity!

Primitive

Willful intervention ruins the harmony
Of the natural conversion process;
The spontaneous rhythm of the primitive equality;
The un-self-conscious symbiosis with Nature's cycles.
Everything is fundamentally one, the whole.
The Supreme Master resides inside all,
And is Superior to all distinction.
Offer no active resistance to person or idea,
To argue, is failing to see the entire total.

Nothing is, named.
Nothing is, said.
Don't meditate.
Don't cognate.
Follow no school.
Follow no way.
Discard knowledge.
Forget distinctions.
Declaring unity creates duality and defiles unity.

Being

Selfless no thought of oneself,
The being knows not to hoard.
With freedom there is no right or wrong,
Near in, behold the great sword.
No way in mind but knowing,
No thought of what's not here.
The doing not thee accomplishments;
Not liking, not disliking, total, and clear;
Oneness with all life, that is.

Filled with the life, power, and love from the void,
Nothing defined, but soft and opaque;
The living void is priceless to one,
With no awareness of oneself,
For the mind, to be graceful and free;
Not I, but the doing,
No effort, but normal.
There's nothing regarded for oneself,
No proceeding, but learning to be.

Passers-By

We're miracles in the mortal,
From the Great God of Love;
Great white pearls, that
Belong to God above.

We're miracles in the mortal,
Pearls stashed in the mud;
Hidden from the one,
That God gave a shove.

We're a light from the Son,
That shines with Love;
We belong to the One,
The Almighty, Lord God above.

Winter

The winter snow is oodles, lot a heap.
Spring is long, late, and cold.
It is said a white horse comes to reap,
Like winter, long, late, and bold.

The spring will be here this I know.
The sap is climbing in the trees.
But now, I am in deep, the snow,
Way up to my knees.

O savage winter, when will you fleet?
Snow flakes, brisk air, freezing rain,
Your bitter bite, cold, and sleet;
How much longer will you remain?

O Spring

O spring,
Where is the beginning that you bring?
Remember your green-spangled garment,
With yellow, purple, and gold!

Awake, and rise from your sleep.
I am longing to meet you there,
Where the vegetation starts to peep,
And the warm air is meek and fair.

O spring, enrich your rain,
And give everyone something to do.
Enrich us all with plenty of grain,
To, make our hearts like new.

Where Are Your Buds

Where are your buds at harvest time?

Are they safe from the sun?

Who shines on all the plots?

Who grows them everyone?

No buds can be complete,

Until they're in the pail to stay;

Let's make a bucket with the tarp,

This harvest day!

Gardener's Poem

Tell me not,
It's time to go.
Into the night
With awe and hoe.

Hollowed, void,
Dark and vast.
Help me not,
Remember the past?

Insects and frogs,
The perching owls sing.
Strolling through grasses
And weeds that sting!

Smacking mosquitoes,
Frights and fears;
Hope in, there in,
There'll be a good year.

Footprints so lite,
Pathless and free,
The Gardener's quest
And place to be.

Into the night
With all its woe;
Please God help me?
It's time to go.

The Season Of Harvest

The season of harvest is here,
With its joints and beer;
When buds and birds are over us,
There is no need to fear.

The season of harvest is here,
We can smell it each day.
There's no time like harvest,
To practice the non-attachment way!

The season of harvest is here,
Surrounded by the buds it brings.
Now weight is in the making,
Can one day spend the things!

The season of harvest is here,
And as we pick buds far and wide;
We should thank God for his blessings,
And hope that he may abide.

Buds Everyone

Plant on the bank,
Share a spot of mine,
To think there's so much for us,
Buds so very fine!

I planted my favorite seeds
And spared them all;
To an empty pocket,
So buds may grow tall.

From the tiny little plant,
Dressed in garden clothes,
To autumn,
When sweet stickiness flows!

Fall!
With all its buds and fun;
Fall is in the air,
Buds everyone!

The Skunk Of Harvest

The skunk of harvest,
Lingers heavy in the air;
Before the wind will change,
It will linger everywhere!

The skunk of harvest,
Working in the humble hype;
With fluffy buds that reek,
And are freshly ripe!

The skunk of harvest,
The smell stays around.
Where the buds are ripening,
And grow up from the ground.

And so it is harvest,
That the nose smells anew.
The cold air of harvest,
Buds from seeds old and new!

The Harvest Season

The harvest season is here,
The smells fill the air.
Airplanes are flying, birds are singing,
Buds are everywhere!

The harvest is a golden time,
Showered by summers love.
The place to make a simple rhyme,
To plants golden Bud above.

Soon the plants will be hanging,
Their presence fills the air.
Laughter and happiness
Are smelt here and there.

For harvest is a happy point,
Expressed by my giving style;
So wrap and lick each joint,
With a loving pile!

Soon you will be singing,
Soon you will come to a restful night.
When the gardener lies sleeping,
Wrapped in sticky buds golden plight.

The Little Seed

There was a little seed,
Hidden in the magic vase,
And though small, dark, and striped,
It has found its place.

Placed in a spot for counting,
A must and don't mind.
Placed very cheaply,
There so kind.

In spite of the suns affection,
Hardy loves it hardy.
And very often,
There's one that's tardy.

So it's on its journey,
Bound for the distant skies,
And from the hand the little seed,
The little one that tries!

But when they reached the sky,
The little one was hardly found;
It stood there in a plot,
That stood there so sound.

Marijuana Plant

I look upon the marijuana plant,
Such beauty does abound.
God gave us the marijuana plant,
A seed too if found.

A plant with unity,
Peace and love.
From the bottom to the top,
It grows to the sun above.

God adorned the marijuana plant
Sparkling bright;
The sun shines upon its branches,
To see the rays of light!

It stands with hope,
And over the plants place,
A scene for the sun,
Free to shine with grace.

It's the season,
With the sun it will grow.
This is the reason,
To plant well to flow!

We gather the buds,
A story rings.
The marijuana plant we celebrate,
To, harvest its things.

The Guide

Planted in the land,
A plant grew into view.
Held there by earths hand,
That stood more than a few.

It guided the gardener traveling
From a different plot,
To feed the plants over yonder,
Across the lot!

Every year they guide him still,
To till around the plants far and wide;
Where the heart must find the will,
To, sow seeds where the shade cannot hide.

All We Are And Can Be

Standing with the arms stretched up,
Wondering about the potential inside;

Wondering if there's a key for the cup,
To unlock the treasures that hide.

Treasures so powerful, gifts of own,
Gifts of art, music, poetry, to heal, to be;

Right or wrong, no divisions are shown,
To make known all we are and can be.

In A Plot

In a plot,
The seeds were placed.
Nestled in the richest earth,
No, matter what they faced.

The old vegetation was sidelined,
Quiet, careful, and seen;
The garden-tool was digging,
The dogs bark on scene.

Maybe in the night,
There'll shine stars.
Rays of light
And silence, few cars.

In a plot the gardener stood,
Holding garden-tool, great worth,
And sometimes food,
To place in the earth.

In a plot,
The place for bets,
No matter what happens,
There'll be no regrets.

Right and wrong,
In God's image we are;
The divisions are,
We are what we are.

We divide, bind n' scar,
To place limits on all we are.
We're so tiny the angels laugh.
Our potential how far?

The things we like,
Then we say they're wrong.
The things we love n' hate,
Then we say they don't belong.

The dreams n' thoughts,
We love n' despise.
The images we mask,
To, demise.

Time

Time is like a shark,
To stop is to die.
Time for the dark,
The darkness and why;
Time is existence in the world,
To endure what we are;
Where the darkness is hurled,
To be hurled far.

Time is a grace,
Good, bad, hard, and not;
The time to embrace,
The time that we got;
Time to take,
The hour of death;
Time enduring, consecrated to make,
The most of each breath!

Time is eternity,
Divisible without end;
The cocoon for maturity,
And the One to, defend.
Time is absolute or relative,
Continuous and unbound;
Feed on the positive,
Where, time is found.

Freedom from greed is freedom from time.

My Return To Nothingness

My way is no way.
There is no joy.
There is no merry heart,
And I cannot accept my works.
My garments are not white,
And I lack oil.
There is no wife in my life of vanity.
There is no portion in my life.
My empty life, I have no might.
There is no work, nor device, nor knowledge,
And there is no wisdom in the grave where I go.
I am not swift, nor strong, nor wise,
I have no riches, nor understanding,
I have no favor, nor skill,
And I know not my time,
My evil time and chance;
Waiting with patience, and with no patience,
For the snare of death and the final judgment!

A Little Spark Of Light

Looking at all the days I recall,
Here in this world, where the mortal must fall.
Out of steam and not so strong,
Woe to my heart, where evil does not belong.
In the dark, the fall from gleam, where,
Somehow, darkness has fastened itself in our dream.

Here:
Just a thought in the dark, a light shines low,
A little spark of light, that surely must know;
Though our heart must be cautious, humble, and strong;
Remembering always to look where we go,
And that only Love, will last along.

Everyday Love, wants us for,
A place in our heart, forevermore;
Our ways may falter, straight is the way,
To be still and listen, who knows the day?
Remember the end, the mortal must fall,
Where Love, is found, the greatest of all.

Weeding

Gliding through the hesitation,
Stomping on the lack of will;
Standing confident for the presentation,
Just a hop and jump over the hill.
The will is strong, until it's time to go,
Then it's too easy, to just say no.
Whatever the cost may be, remember the fall;
Whatever it takes to see, you can have it all.
The prizes may appear farther than they are.
The days get brighter and not so far.
To the very best, you have all winter to rest,
But now the test!
Think of all the variety, beauty, and weight,
Remembering to weed, and how they can't wait.

Hold your hoe and you'll go far.
Don't get caught, or you'll be a scar.
Patches so fruitful and deep;
Patches so plentiful to reap;
Patches hard to beat;
Patches placed so neat.
Just maybe there'll be some disbelief,
But if you work real hard and do what you know;
You can have it all, with no grief.
Pick up the feet, protect the eyes,
Where, things in the dark are in disguise.
The sore hands, the feet,
A coronary abrasion,
To the weedy invasion!

My Confession

My past I hold before me,
Belief stricken with the sight;
And I, the Nature that be,
Am in dirt with little might!

I confess, I am in a pigpen,
Defiled earth and parasites;
Expected to stay clean then,
While scratching the miserable mites!

In your image,
For what I am and love;
Lead to feel guilty,
To, being lead by the tail with a shove.

Given all the thoughts and desires,
An Ego, that requires.
Thank you for all the experience, once again,
And I thank you again and again, now and then.

Nature's Song

Strolling through the wilderness wild,
Listening to the songs that be;
Along the river wild,
O how it sings to me.

The hymn of the gentle wind!
The blue jays and robins sang their tune.
The squirrels joined in,
And the humming bird in early June.

Singing their happy songs,
Free and clear.
The loon joined in and belongs,
How I, love to hear.

The larking coyote does aspire,
To the happy songs;
Overhead an eagle's cry with fire,
In accord to all the songs.

O how I love to hear the wild,
Listening to the songs that be;
Along the river wild,
O how it sings to me.

I Hold Within My Heart

Alone inside I wait,
Free from the raging sea.
I see my plight or fate,
The heaven, that's inside of me.
I hold within my heart a place,
Undivided and not apart to see;
A secret place to embrace,
The peace that is a part of me!

I'm awake night and day,
My enemies are seeking me.
They wish to make me astray,
Apart of their destiny!
Evil knows their own,
They eagerly seek me;
They will leave their own alone,
In pursuit after me!

Goodness brought me to a great height,
An eternal throne;
A soul of pure light,
And wisdom of re-own!
From evil I have fled,
Into an open door;
From those which are dead,
To, undivided, Love, forevermore.

The Ladder To Heaven

I hide my heart in the beginning,
There it will be safe to the end.

The soul will return to the beginning,
In which is the end.

A billion steps descend,
A billion steps ascend.

From Heaven we climb down,
To Heaven, we climb the same steps going back up.

Beware the steps down,
And remember, the same steps go back up.

The Essence

Our mind is very complex

And everything is from the essence.

We should be cautious what we fashion

And how that we conclude.

The free mind is not, divided by anything or law.

To choose choices, that is positive in the now,

To be justified by faith, in Immanuel Jesus, His example.

The mind is where the thoughts are.

Choose the positive and choose life,

To be free from the negative fancy torments of Hell.

Only negativity would lead in fear.

Negativity can have a positive form.

Those closest to the fire, are closest to the Lord.

Split the wood, and there He is.

A Place To Remember

Among the hails in the storms,
Implanted those fears of God,
To gain, to manipulate their reforms;
Where darkness n' evils are.
Where hearts n' roses; will leave a scar.
A deceitful journey that's dark and dangerous;
Where doubt is only doubt,
And fear is only to be feared.
A place to remember,
Only God is to be loved and revered.

Unfortunate Reality

All is ready,
I'm ready to show.
To the shop,
Where, some may go.

For each and all,
There's no wonder.
Short or tall,
To rest asunder.

Well built vaults,
Built with care;
Not your faults,
Life's fare!

But if the vault
You can't earn.
There are other spaces,
You may urn.

Holy Smokes

The lungs are full of smoke today,

I heard the music sing.

The pipe I cleared a way,

For the bag of buds to bring!

Their smoke filled the air,

The airways coughed clear.

The goober hacked away,

To the gifts of cheer!

Christmas Gift Cat

This cat likes to play night or day,
It has its way.
To and fro, it wants to go,
All hours, I'm sure she'll show.

This cat con's like a stray,
Her tiny painful voice ask to be let out,
Before I get there, she'll playfully run away;
She'll repeat it a lot without a doubt.

I haven't been rough to her,
She's a nice cat, at least she were.
Her voice is tiny and it even hurts the ear,
It shouldn't take long, to see and hear.

Every once and awhile,
She'll sneeze!
I hate it when this happens on my lap or knees,
So, if she leans back, cover your eyes and don't smile.

This cat loves to hunt for prey.
She'll catch a butterfly in mid air,
Then make it her day.
I hope she'll find butterflies there.

I've never even given this cat a name;
She appears calm and tame.
Although, she has a tiny little frame,
I'm sure she'll love you the same.

A Plea

I know time is moving on,
The seconds are passing by.
With every day that passes on,
Please God, help us try.
Your spirit is here and there,
Inside and out;
Take away our feelings of despair
And all our doubt.
Remember our enemies and bless them first
And remember us, before the Hurst.
Give us all your gifts of grace,
To hold all of us in your heart,
Our own peaceful place.

The Birthday Poem

To my little kid,
I love with care.
I love you the most
And will always be there.

Through the years,
Good times and tears.
I'll take your frights
And your fears!

Band-aid on sores,
Or random chores;
The love I have for you,
Like an ocean, that has no shores.

Rockin

Ah! Now you're here,
The day is done.
You drink your beer,
Ah! You have one.
You can do what you want,
You can let it go.
If it is music you want, then,
Welcome to the show!

The lights are on;
The sound is clear.
The rhythms are on, and
Rockin' is here.
What's on your mind?
O it's a wild night;
Don't ever stop the,
Rockin' all night!

So open your ears, and
Turn on the noise, we'll
Rock this place, and
Shatter it with noise!
We'll let it go,
We'll give it our all.
Rockin' the show,
Rockin' you all!

The sweat is pouring;
The heat is on;
The atmosphere is soaring, and
Rockin' is on!
All you hear is rhythms;
We love it loud;
The beat is on,
So, Rock it out loud!
No matter what you do,
No matter where you go;
It will be comin' at you,
Just lettin' you know!
The beat will be hard,
The rhythm in blue;
Rockin' hard,
Rockin' you!

Usefulness

People that are useful,
Toil in a daily grind.
They labor and are wrathful,
And some loose their mind.

A tree carries much fruit,
Or it does not.
It labors all summer,
Then it's plundered and got.

Useful, broken, and barren,
Robbed with nothing to share;
Can you see therein?
How it's fair.

Useless things are happy,
Great usefulness in uselessness it seams;
Look at the knurled useless tree that is happy,
Resting by the stream.

Returning Misfortunes

You send me your hate,
You give me your pain;
Is this just fate?
You call out my name!

You send me a curse,
You give me shame;
Is there anything worse?
Or is this just fame?

You lie, cheat, and steal,
You throw smoke, stones, and sand;
How does it feel?
You take your last stand!

You imagine my misfortunes,
You cast me your spells;
All the misfortunes,
On your own head they fell.

So don't send me a curse,
A bloody spell!
It just may reverse,
And send you through Hell!

The Monarch

There are two sides with everything:
Right and left; joy and sorrow;
Up and down; love and hate;
Good and evil; earth and water,
The Yin and Yang!
Only when we find the One, centered
Between the two,
Can we achieve Greatness?
In perfect Unity, Peace, and Balance,
Body-Mind-Soul!

If we can find the Universal Mind, the Monarch,
We would all live as one.
The Trinity—becoming one in Essence.
Animal becoming Man,
Man becoming Deity.
The Mortal—is an Enemy of the Immortal?
Matter is subject to Regeneration.
The Essence of Mind, is Immeasurable—
Invisible-Eternal-Ineffable!
Reposing in Silence, no one Lords over it.

I Can

I can jump on the sun,
I can glide to the moon;
I can catch a ride on the jet stream,
And be back by noon.

I can float over the prairie,
I can rest on a tree;
I can visit the Grand Canyon,
And be back by three.

I can travel on a wave,
I can mount the birds;
I can fly to the edge of a cave,
Painting pictures with words.

I can run to the Mountains,
I can fish by a stream;
I can visit Mt. Everest,
And still see the stream.

I can visit the past,
A thought away;
I can stand by a ship's mast,
And hang out for the day.

The Wolf

A creature of instinct, it runs alone, or in packs—
Packs led by the alpha, the hierarchy of the pack.
From Yellowstone to the Rockies,
To Alaska to the Northern Plains States it roams.

The wolf is majestic and powerful—
The pups are born in the spring.
The pups are raised by the entire pack,
To teach, to give them nurturing.

Resting, or running with pace—
Their noses fixed toward the wind.
Their eyes set toward the horizon,
They can see, sense, and hear everything.

Intelligent and social—
The wolf mates for life, the two—
It weeds out the less fit, stalks and chases
Mice, rabbits, birds, deer, moose, and caribou!

The wolf sits upon the high ground—
It howls into the moon-lit wind,
It travels here, there, and all around,
It rarely accepts an interloper within.

Feathers By The Stream

Wandering through the woods at bay,
Gathering feathers,
The crow—
The hawk—
The woodpecker—the blue jay;
To, place them in a vase to stay.
Oh, how I,
Love the feather bouquet.

The windy breeze—
The chipmunks sing—
The clear air—
The water blings;
Oh, the feathers I seize,
The stories ring,
Traveling through the woods,
Wandering!

Cool-wind gusts from the West.
The walnuts—
The acorns are falling from the trees—
The mice—the squirrels—
The chipmunks build their nest—
The leaves and feathers,
Floating in the breeze, collecting
Feathers by the stream!

The Summer's End

The summer was long and short,
The days were hot and often dry.
The spring had arrived early
And now it has all moved on by.

The robins—the blue jays—
The early buds on the trees—
The green grass—the clear sunny days—
The bumble bees and green leaves.

The frogs singing in the swales,
The light or dark nights, under the stars.
The crickets—the lightning bugs' glowing tails—
The gardens and the yard!

The warm n' calm or cool-breezy days n' nights,
The airplanes and clouds passing over the moon;
The sunlight reflecting the moon n' stars, lights
The night like noon!

And then the fall, the cold-wind blast,
That makes the weeds n' trees bend;
The summer never lasts,
The summers end.

The Sacred Heart

(Inspired by Mother Teresa)

The Sacred Heart, who can explain?
A deep devotion of unselfish sacrifice and pain;
To feed, cloth, shelter, and nurse the sick—
The outcast—the dying—the unloved,
Those who suffer lost faith and all hope!
The poorest of the poor
And the lowest of the low;
Gods closest suffer to endure.
The homeless in the streets, slums, and the ghetto;
Suffering hunger, tuberculosis, leprosy, and polio—
Faith in prayer, love, service, and peace;
For the Love of God,
Endures all humiliation and suffering;
Free of personal bias and self-sacrificing!

The Light

Life is mean
And the days get hard . . .
A world of schemes,
The bitter and scared . . .

So, when life is rue,
The good or bad . . .
Like, the dark-mean streets, to
The dreams that make you glad . . .

Look deep into your heart,
In through your eyes,
To see the Light that lights the start,
Then reach for the skies . . .

And when life is all right,
Above the broken rue, that makes you happy or blue,
Remember the Light
And it will guide you through.

The Harrowing Voyage

(Inspired by the Edmond Fitzgerald)

As dusk darkened into night
Sailing on an open sea
Guided by the stars
The time goes by
Riding on a wave
Sailing the heavy seas

A gale blowing in the face
Pushing through the raging sea
The hatches closed
Ringing full speed ahead
On past the safety of the lee
Amid the din of high wind and seas

The Master in the pilothouse
Making his scheme and run
Navigating through snow squalls, fog, and limited visibility
Sailing into the rising-whirling sea
A promise on time
Charting destiny

Taking a pounding—a flawed plan
Giant waves cleared the bow
A monster storm or fate
Sailing full speed ahead through the savage wind and seas
A nor'easter gale built to a size who could believe
Into the blackness of the deep sea

The hours tic away
Pushing the RPM
Looking for shelter or the safety of a lee
It's a matter of time
The terrible weather and huge seas
Pure confusion—the quartering sea
Struggling on through the storm
A helluva place out on the open sea
Forever in the moment the fateful voyage
Sailing those treacherous seas
Forever in time
Sailing into a wave to eternity

Loneliness

Loneliness' pain is more painful than hunger
And everyday I dreamed of thy love—
Where the Soul does wander,
Mid the painful longings that flow like blood.
Everyday the pain I do meet,
It wanders far and wide—
Everyday it wanders amid these feet,
Rejected at the heart of Pride—
Everyday I long to greet,
Though still denied!

Death Alone

In the fading days of isolation and naught—
Dwells the soul alone and still.
Ever bleak and taught—
Timid and suffering and nil!

Death calls—
My greatest friend—
Silence and peace alike—enthralls
The greatest end!

Heaven is so rich—
Poverty is all that lack.
The wealth—the power—the hitch—
Lord, for the 'Love of God', I give it all back.

The Source Of Life

The source of all Life,
Weak and yielding as water,
That overcomes the hard and strong,
And always takes low ground.
Develop the male and female equal,
But prefer femininity.
Feed from the Holy Mother,
And find the well that never runs dry.
Find the Empty Center,
Work reflexively, without conscious intent.

Bondage To Freedom

Bondage is a spirit that clings to form.
A spirit that refuses to reform;
And is any spirit that does not live through sacred example.
Even Jesus said, who I set free, is free indeed.
To the free, their hearts and minds are ample,
Not by being ample, but by, not being ample.

Making room for example, through sacred example;
Reforming not to cling to form, where truth is, formless.
There is a right and wrong,
But to be bound by right or wrong,
Is not singing any joyous song,
Yet, with joy comes cessation.

To pick up any stone,
Is to carry the weight and the stone;
To be free,
The stone must be thrown.
Being total
And free.

The Everlasting Chain

Here in this heart of mine,
I feel you and see your face.
Burning in this chest of mine,
The thoughts of you, I love to embrace.
Early on, you pierced my heart
And my soul does believe.
I dream about you from the start,
How I dream of holding you all night to perceive.

Trembling with passion—swollen and hard,
The stars—a moon,
A screech owl in yard;
You've always been here in this heart of mine,
I love you so, from so long ago.
Every year that goes on by,
You've been here in my heart;
I can only wonder why.

What heartbreak to have love and not love
And only in dreams do embrace.
What a tragedy to never hold the one you love,
What misfortune—what chance?
What a curse to go through life knowing and not knowing,
Having love and never being with the one you love.
The thoughts of you and me together,
Bliss in paradise forever.

You touched me with love and planted a seed of lasting love.
It is you I will always remember.
Staring at these thoughts of you,
Planted here in my heart, by you;
All the desires—all the dreams,
I've seen all the pain this world can bring.
It is you in my heart, I cannot fling,
You are beautiful, more beautiful than everything.

Night Snap

Night Snap:
Will leave you nothing but a morn,
Leave you nothing, to creep, through the darkness and corn!
Many years, I grew amongst the very best.
And every year, Night Snap,
From North, South, East, and West!
Many a night,
I beg—I plead,
God, don't let them take the rent.
It wasn't very often, that I didn't get bent.

In the fall, a ripe scent fills the air.
In the fall, bets are here and there.
In the fall, hopes are high.
And in the fall, there's always a wonder why?
A wonder why?
They don't grow their own.
A wonder why?
They take what I sown.
And then there's Karma,
They should have known.

Thinking nobody is watching, they dare.
Not realizing that I and the dead are there.
The stolen treasure is so sweet,
And then there's the Law of Compensation, they do meet.
Meeting their indiscretions of injudiciousness, they do pay.
Here I realize, maybe they don't know the way.
A way that is easier, to grow their own;
To know where to look, their very own;
A place where they can finish, to a good yield,
To the weediest place, maybe somewhere around a field!

Don't be lazy, heart and guts.
Where, sometimes, a place may require big nuts!
Seeking accomplishments at hand,
To weed, feed, and till,
Like a phantom, ever so smooth and still!
To handle every plant, as innocent as a dove,
In return, they will give you the greatest love.
Love so great, you'll fill every bucket,
And if you fill every bucket,
You may need to truck it.

Childlike

To be restricted to one's own assumptions—
Is a conclusion within oneself!
As in loving one's own image—an Illusion—
In which—we attach our self.

A bird can perch in the bitter cold—
A fish can swim in the open sea—
The poet sings songs new and old,
O' how much this cosmos—has for you and for me.

The body has limits—
The Mind is unrestricted—
To expand—to free our consciousness,
Is the Power of Greatness—within you and me!

A Winter's Wonderland

The night is peaceful and beautiful.
Mesmerized by the thick falling snow flakes,
That makes the snow-laden branches bend—
A winter's wonderland!

The moon rises at midnight.
A cold, blustery, February night,
Among the subzero, snow storming polar planet—
The heavy wet snow.

Nestled by the warm blazing woodstove fire,
The red-hot coals pop.
Hearing the din of howling wind whistle—
Whistling, high-pitched and low!

The rising whirling snow piles deep and grows.
The deep blanket of snow sparkles and glows.
Watching the storming, heavy, wet snows—
Feeling, the winter's freezing subzero below.

The trails are snow drifted and locked down.
As the raging snow blows and whirls around,
To the chest the snow does stand—
A winter's wonderland!

The Call

Wandering through the pouring rain,
Rain-soaked and cold through the storm, traveling.
Alone and soaked, shivering in pain.
Sensing someone is following.
Roaming through life alone,
It is God who is following, to bring you home.
Ever patient and persistent,
His love is faithful and ever present.

God follows to be followed.
He is here to seek and save the lost.
He sees in you something hollowed,
To Him you are beautiful and sparkle as the frost.
His thirst for your love and to love is great.
He gives you His gifts of love.
He gives you His Holy Ghost, as harmless as a dove.
He loves you just the way you are.

He gives you Michael, Raphael, Gabriel, and Uriel.
He sends His Guardian Assistance with might.
He gives you free will.
He will move mountains and oceans with one call.
He will empty your cup to fill.
He will pick you up when you fall.
His burden is Light.
He will light the way, to guide you home.

Cause And Effect

(Inspired by the Dalai Lama)

Being aware of the consciousness of mind,
Like the conditions that give rise to results.
Nothing remains static or permanent.
The habit forming conscious mind can change.
We can change the attitudes and emotions.
We can transform our state of mind—
Nurturing love diminishes hate,
Nurturing friendliness diminishes unfriendliness.
Changing the mind from an afflictive condition,
To a mind that is in a non-afflictive position.

Mental Energy

Facing the morning rising sun,
To slowly breathe in deeply
All of the positive forces in Nature;
And then, slowly exhale the entire negative from within.
Then when you are full of positive energy,
You can direct your Mental Energy, toward the ailment.

Awaiting Spring

I'm waiting for spring, to work in the garden.
Awaiting the sent of rich-moist soil—
The cool and warm weather—
The birds sing as,
The sun's cresting over the horizon.
Time is mine, camping, fishing, hunting feathers.

I'm free to do as I please.
The things I love, such as these.
Planting trees and vegetable seeds—
The English walnut—the peach—the pear—
The plum—the hazelnut—the chestnut trees—
I'm planting the fruitful variety, such as these.

The strawberries—the boysenberry—
The raspberry—the blackberries and grapes—
To take time off—fishing and camping.
The time goes past—time is naught.
Watching things grow fast—
A great price, my freedoms been bought.

The Lady In Paradise

There is a beautiful lady in Paradise.
A blissful delight she is.
She has a clear voice, soft, kind, and lovely.
She was cutting rutabaga for rutabaga pudding.
"Surprising!" she said,
"My husband eats two bowls everyday for lunch."

A Portrait

Light Green Rolling Mountain pastures.
Overhead, a blue sky and small-puffy-white clouds formed.
Over yonder a large thundering heard of mustangs, running fro.
A lite breeze—the grasshoppers fly.

A Positive

Lightning cannot harm Lightning.

Lightning needs a Negative Ground, to ark.

A Positive ark cannot harm unless there is a Negative.

A Positive cannot harm a Positive.

A Positive will consume a Negative.

A Positive will not harm itself.

Blessed is a soul that eats the Positive to become Man.

Cursed is a soul that the Positive eats to become Man.

Man

Man is distinguished from all other animals.
His is sense of strength.
He is human and divine being.
He is vigor.
He is bravery.
He has magnanimity.
He is master of his mental powers.
He has control of his actions.
He is free from the dictates of another.
He is the highest degree beyond all other.
He is best known to himself.
He will overcome to defeat.

"Name of God: in the Scriptures, the titles, attributes, word, wisdom, power, works, will, goodness, or glory of God himself" =[Man].

A King

"As above, so below
As within, so without"
—The Emerald Tablet, circa 3000 BC

His power is awareness of power.
His heart and mind are one.
He is High Minded.
He Trust no one.
He learns to be alone.
He will concur all.
He will rule all.
He is one with all.
He let's all conflict cease.
He accomplishes the greatest deeds.
His will is His own.
His word will be known.

His will is His birthright.
His will is all that is His.
He will bless His enemies.
He will bless all that is.
He will be motivated by love and love Himself.
He is because He is.
He directs His will.
He will remember to remember.
He is master of the Universe.
He wills positively.
His is understanding, grace, perception, and perfection.
His home is Silence.

A Gig From In High

Our Eternal Souls would not understand the value of their eternal beings without experiencing opposites and death.

It is, understanding opposites and death that gives us Eternal Souls the knowledge, wealth, diversity, and the value of Eternal Life.

Eternity is a long time,
We Souls need to do something with our Minds.

I wonder what 'Will' be next.

The Magic Mountains

A Great Heavenly Journey, to a Great Coast—approaching the Magnificent Magic Mountains—a fly down toward the Eastern horizon—a kingdom—soaring—the sky is full of beautiful splendor—illuminate—ecstasy—as like seeing through an Eagle's eye—total bliss in silence—paradise.

The Most Important

By being wrapped up in our daily lives, we let go the most important gift in life, the family—we lose the love from those who nurture us and give us peace, guidance, and homage—
Living is the time to create good memories; memories of family should be more than at a funeral.

The Sun Is Always Shining

The sun is always shining—
Some things are sometimes flip—
Give it a single blessing,
The blessing will provide the flip.

Sometimes there are Majestic Mountains—
Sometimes there are Wind and Sea—
Sometimes there are Days of Wandering,
But never are you apart from me.

Each and every moment is a new day—
Every day is the same way—
There is only bliss in Heaven,
I will you there to stay.

Late February

It is a bitter-cold February morning—still.
You could hear a bird's nest fall from a tree a mile away.
The passing clouds are gray and few.
The quiet trees are bare—tranquil.

It is a late winter—a little snow.
You can see the dormant weeds.
A lite dusting of snow peppers the ground.
The birds are unmoving—the rooster cries.

It is a glorious morning—peaceful.
You can smell the arrival of spring's fresh air.
The sun is below the horizon, but light.
The Chipmunks turn in their hibernation—ready to emerge.

Heart And Mind

Strolling through the trails of life,
Seeing all the different ways—
Thinking all ways lead to life,
Realizing the Sacred Heart leads the way.
The mind may differ,
But the heart will choose.
When the mind is ruled by the Sacred Heart,
One cannot lose.

A Son Of Kings

Wandering through the land of the devouring serpent,
On foot from beginning to end—
Standing alone in a lonely land,
Set in a dream, I am,
Caught in a wilderness roaming;
Fixed in a delusion, I stand;
Endless miles of traveling,
Suffering beneath the yoke of slavery.

Wandering through the land of the devouring serpent,
I tasted their food—
I fell into a deep sleep;
A Son of Kings in a desperate land,
A wicked wilderness of pain;
Listening for the voice I recognize,
The King of Kings,
Suffering beneath the yoke of slavery.

Wandering through the land of the devouring serpent,
Looking for the pearl—
The stolen pearl from my Father's palace;
A little child girded with steel.
Roaming from my homeland in the East,
Looking for my kinsmen for company;
In a far-off land they dealt treacherously with me,
Suffering beneath the yoke of slavery.

Passion

Jesus, I will to play with you by the stream,
To gather flowing waters into pools
And make them immediately pure.
I will to order it by speaking a single word.

With you I will to make some soft mud
And fashion twelve sparrows from it,
To clap my hands and cry to the sparrows "Be gone!"
I will to be righteous and kind.

In you, I will to be like you, to bear leaves and root and fruit.
I will to go further on my way.
I will that everything I say is deed accomplished.
I will to bless and to curse.

I will to speak the word, and bear my reward.
For everything I say in you, whether good or bad,
To, become an amazing reality,
To act wisely and to seek and to find, I am yours.

I will to be a bright servant with a good mind.
I will to know the true nature of the Alpha and the Beta.
I will to not be of this world, to even tame fire.
I will to follow your reasoning.

I will to be your student, and to have you as my teacher.
My friend, I will to be able to look into your face.
I will to know the beginning and the end.
Bring me back home, to know your Greatness.

Now let what is mine bear fruit,
And let my blind heart see.
I will to be from above to bless them and to curse them,
And call them to the realm above.

In you,
I will to stand alone,
You have raised me up.
I will to glorify God and worship Jesus.

I will to force my way through the crowd,
To grab all that has been struck, to be healed.
I will to rise,
And remember you, for, the Spirit of God, to live within me.

I will to sow a single grain of wheat,
To, produce a hundred large bushels.
To feed the poor,
And to give my family what is left of it.

Show me the power of the Alpha and the Beta.
Allow me to speak in the Holy Spirit.
Allow me to speak with great beauty.
Fill me with great grace and wisdom.

I will to be rightly spoken, and to be a rightly borne witness.
I will you to breathe on humanities bite from the snake,
For the pain to, be immediately stopped.
For the snake to, burst, and for life to return to health.

Free

I'm going to the wild,
To plant some skunk and cheese;
I'm growing in the night,
Where I can be free;
So, on my own,
So many directions;
It is so lovely,
Through the deepest weeds,
Under the starlight,
Where, my seeds will be sown.

I'm going to the wild,
I find myself in different places.
I find my love,
The greatest feeling,
So, on my own;
So many different ways,
When moving through the Wild,
My greatest love under the starlight,
Sets me free;
Where, my seeds will be grown.

I'm going to the wild,
It's so lovely.
Where the frogs and crickets sing,
The shadows, the silhouette of trees;
A night in the wild,
Making memories,
Where I am home,
In the Wild with all of these;
The Wild wilderness of the Night,
Where, I can be free.

Home In The Wild

Home in the wild,
Where Indians and Settlers roam—
At home in the Northern Woodlands,
A place I call home.

The Beach—the Birch—the Black Walnut—
Edibles the frontiersmen have known.
The Blueberries—the Gooseberries—the Currants—
Fruits the North American Bushmen have well-known.

Home in the wild,
Home in the majestic woods,
Where edibles abound—
My favorite Wild North American Woodlands.

Living in the forest,
The greatest of all—
Primitive conditions—
Where, every necessity is free.

At home in the wild,
Living off the land, staying alive—
Shelter for the making—
A warm fire lights the night time sky.

The animals—the trees—the vegetation—
There's always a way.
At home in the North American Untamed Woodlands,
A place I call home.

Undaunted

A low-lying mist,
Wandering on a path through the deep dense woods—
The fog refused to lift,
The rain and mist blurred the trail ahead.

Searching for the sun through a break in the clouds,
A fair-weather oasis—
A gentle breeze—
The green pastures around the deep blue sea.

Like a sparrow gliding through thin air over rugged cliffs—
Undaunted—
Turning toward the sun, there's tranquility ahead,
Where, the light is serene.

The Demon Encounter

Once upon a time,
There was a puzzled Demon.
The Demon was crawling toward me down in a trench.
It had razor sharp teeth and pointed ears.
It was crawling close to the ground upon its hands and feet.
The creature was timid.
It was lurking toward me looking up and was afraid.
And with the power of my mind,
I jumped upon the Demon.
And as I was upon it,
I gave it a loving hug and a kiss from Unconditional Love.
I have not seen it since.

Nature's Heart

Alive in the wild,
A peaceful and untamed wilderness deep in the forest—
The cool winds gently whisper through the timber.
A calm brook, babbling stream, and Northern lights—
The summer night's sky!
Home with the divine, timber wolves, bear, and eagle.
Forest souls my friends in the Northern wilderness of the Wild.
Where, Nature's heart tampers the will.

Haunting howls echo through the silent night.
The wolves acknowledge the coming of winter.
The great horned owl hoots as the crickets cry.
A gentle breeze—
Wild nights and days in the back country—
The cool Northern Lakes echo the forest souls.
The Rambling River and wood frogs plop.
The song birds sing from Nature's heart.

The Gardener's Scheme

He fills his bowl with cheese.
He lights a flame, for the smoke to display.

A little hash in his bowl with cheese,
The smoke rolls array.

He looks out into his cheese filled garden plot.
All his girls bow and wave.

He is a gardener with a green thumb and magic touch.
He has a garden tool and knack that make plants grow.

He has a couple roosters and hounds to guard the bunch.
And all the people that come and go say hello.

I Am One

I'm leaving this bloody world of suffering.
I overcame the Dragon—the Beast,
That smashed my brain.
I'm leaving this bloody body—I overcame.
I am not my body, mind, or will.
I am because I am.
I will remain the same.
I came I triumph I reign.

I made the world to shake.
I am Unconditional Love.
I am here to destroy the Curse of the Snake,
And to, bring you to the, Lord above.
At last my time is here.
I am one, covered in blood.
Mine is Legion, and aye, I Love you and remove your fear.
I am a Universal Monarch—I Am One.

The Opening Day

The sun rises above the misty hill,
And the mighty trees stand eerily still—
Still, silence among the musty air,
A great white-tailed buck is standing there.
Silence breaks as the blue-jays sing,
And a feather falls from its moving wing.
The rising breeze, from its flight displayed,
Floating through the timber its feather was laid.
Timid, with a silent moan,
Stand the white-tail's ears, as it stands there alone.

The mist rises above the golden hill-side,
Then it's the white-tail's quest for a place to hide.
Where there's brush and thorn and ferns—
Where there's the cover of gold leaves the white-tail yearns.
Among the safety of the foliage of cover,
Where the white-tail rests as a raven fly's over.
Above, the raven does fly high,
Then its deadly call makes an eerie cry.
Open to the predator's hand,
The white-tail's living in a dangerous land.

Among the brush and thorn and fern as still as stone,
Dwells the white-tail perfectly still and alone,
Ever silent—a flick of its tail,
Amid its secret home of hidden vale.
And over its place a squirrel is building,
Its nest with little twigs extending,
In an oak tree, by the gentle creek,
The woodpecker is pecking and hammering its beak.
And beneath the tree a chipmunk bolted and rent,
Under the dry leaves the year fled and went.

Behold The Light

Everything is from nothing.
And from nothing everything is.
So if you want something revisit nothing,
And behold, there it is.
The mind is a sword.
Says a Child of Light,
So with the Power of Will, say the Magic Word,
And Behold the Light.

A Fall Day

Above the fair and peaceful autumn field,
Gray-blue clouds pass across the open sky.
A moment in time for reaping the golden yield,
That sweeps summer's warmth away—as geese fly by.
The red, golden, and brown leaves enthrall.
Amid a short lived cool calm fall day—the blue jays cry.

The Power Of The Prince

Brain power of the mightiest,
Fighting with his will—
Completely relaxed in mind and body,
Beyond all harm,
The mind wills.
The body obeys—the power of the prince,
At home in the low ground, soft and yielding as water,
Abiding and communing with nature.
Pure, perfect, and mysterious,
Accomplishes great things,
For greater spiritual heights in emptiness,
While riding on the blades of a reed.

I Invited A Friend To Heaven

(Inspired by Black Jack)

I invited a friend to Heaven.
A place I call home.
I invited him to, one of my Paradises—
In my Heavenly Father's Kingdom,
I invited him to, come and roam.
And with the White Light of the Holy Ghost, I bless him—
Inside and out I bless him.
And seven hours later, he arrived at my Heavenly Home.

In flashes—he could be and see.
Three o'clock in the morning, his call and testimony.
The magnificence and splendor he could be and see.
I spoke to him without a word, in Silence.
And as he could hear the wolves in the distance, I said,
"Be not afraid!"—I showed him my Glory.
Lightening Fast and a Mighty Will,
Flashes of Light—Impenetrable—Sword and Shield!

Swatting Flies

I walk around my room, swatting flies—
I swat them at rest, or, flying through the open sky.

I swat them to the right; I swat them to the left—
I swat them and they may take flight.

Flying and dive-bombing and buzzing round my head—
Flies land on my nose, while I'm lying on my bed.

Flies flying in, flies never end—
A fly—swatting flies seems like an awful pastime, to spend.

Flies gathered on the window screen—
Flies stuck to the sticky string.

Flies swatted—when I take a stand—
Fly guts smeared across the window, swatter, and hand.

A Way

A way is unspoken and empty,
Purity—not a sound, but a breath.
Sweet silence unbroken,
There, the soul is found breathing free from death.

In The Dark

The gardener is tromping across the wet grassy field,
With stalks in hand and a sticky sweet yield.
The sweat is pouring down his face—
The poor gardener is under the stack without a trace.
Leaves and limbs are in his eye.
Itchy, sweet, sticky, buds, just waiting to get high n' dry.
When he can stick them to a tree,
Then he'll finally be lite and free.

Sitting In The Old Oak Chair

Sitting in the old oak chair,
Trimming buds with cigarette and toxic fumes in air.
Sweet buds and sticky fingers,
Sweet leaf clippings are here and there.
The cars, the planes, the noises everywhere,
Just sitting here trimming—
Trimming buds for the fare.
Sitting in the old oak chair!

The Alpha And The Beta

THE BEGINNING AND THE END
THE LOGOS

Love = Being = Christ = Word = Light = Will =
Thought = Form = Breath =Voice = Speech = Power.

As you speak it, so be it.

The Light Of Day

You can enter the fish in the sea.
You can enter the wolf on the land.
Whatever you will to do or be,
You are grand.

You can soar like a bird.
You can ride the dragon.
Whatever you create with Word,
You can imagine your Heaven.

Everything is a thought away—
Only Love can enter the Light of Day.
So if you cannot find the way.
Rid yourself of everything—to purity.

The Mistress In The Mist

I dreamed I was among a misty forest.
Among the mist a thick vapor of fog,—
Stand a beautiful lady, standing over the bog.
Her radiance shines a pure White Light.
Her pure conscious is radiating her purity bright.
Cloaked in purple with a magic bow, brilliantly tall,
A conqueror, guarding life's gold, from the fall.
Her arrows are Air, Earth, Water, and Fire.

There, at ease, I saw the glory of the Lady.
I was drinking the dew—the mist of life.
Soaring above the throne, intimate with the misty sky—
My name, my name she did silently impress;
Then I was belt with a living shield and sword,
Mighty in strength and flame in eye.

My friend will not forget me, though the mortal will fall.
Although many things are cast into the deep,
A Silent Peace, for all—
And after other's awake from their sleep,
A perfect Paradise, uttered from shore;
And disregard evil, forevermore.
Pure Love, and those dreams to ride,
Through evil, where, her, Great Heart, abide.

I Ask I Believe I Receive

Surround us with the White Light of the Holy Ghost.
Embrace us with warmth and light.
Bless us with beauty, love, and goodness.

Bless us with peace and joy.
Heal us with heat and release.
Bless us with assurance and Divine Power.

Bless us with serenity and tranquility.
Touch us with Christ's healing grace.
Bless us with the power of God.

Bless us with vitality and re-creative energy.
Grant us with life and wholeness and well-being.
Bless us with the greatest faith.

Bless us with prosperity, achievement, and success.
Allow us to visualize, actualize, and realize attainment.
Bless us with positive affirmation.

Bless us with wholesome thoughts.
Bless us with a positive thought pattern.
Bless us with thanksgiving and kindness.

I Am

I AM Pure Love—the Spark in the center of your Soul.
I AM the ALL in ALL, which rules, before thought wills.
I AM the Silent Being,
I AM everything.
I AM everything I Will I AM;
I AM Pure Love.
I AM what I AM that I AM.

Mine Is Power

Mine is Power, I will prevail.
I Believe I Am I Will.

My Mighty Sword and Shield,
I AM Word, Hunting and Fighting Principalities and Powers.

I AM I Will light them up with Electrical Power.
I AM Pure Energy and Static.

I AM All Amps.
Mine is Power, blazing bright in the night.

All Will Be Well

Touch this poem and all will be well.
Believe it in your heart from me.
I give you this poem to reverse the spell
And heal the blind to see—
Might as well and All Will Be Well.
A little touch and you'll be free.

Climbing To The Top Of The Mountain

Climbing to the top of the mountain,
A lonesome feeling with extraordinary obstacles,
Great rockslides, while climbing to the mountain peak,
Up a great gorge—a long climb.
Over masses of immense granite,
Reaching the summit top, where, my native star shines bright.

Across rough terrain—gaining a ridge,
Glistening snow, high in the clouds,
Glacial-polished walls, steep and rugged,
The air is extremely cold and dense.
A giant among giants,
The magnificent mountain is ice clothed and harsh.

Climbing alone,
Gazing at the clouds—a gleam of sun shines through,
The gale force winds and mist and sleet.
Swinging the ice axe in strong wind—a slow ascent,
The terrain is dangerous with loose snow and strenuous.
The storm clouds roll.

Climbing to the top of the mountain,
Among thunder and lightning and the roar of a gale,
The cold is intense.
The summit is waiting.
A fantasy world of rock, wind, and snow,
The powerful gods have their way.

A Trickster Of Kind

(Inspired by Black Jack)

A phantom-magician with rain-boots,
Levitating through the night,
Tapping on the upper window, thrice—on its way it went.
Wearing a trench-coat and top-hat, it had no body.
A phantom levitating off into the night,
It must have been somebody.

I'll never know.
I close my eyes a million times.
I will never know.
A phantom in black,
Into thee abyss, it's in my mind.
It may be back—A trickster of kind.

Virtue

Love
Peace
Wisdom

Courage
Knowledge
Temperance

Patience
Justice
Truth

Hope
Faith
Reason

Healing The Body

Righteous thoughts produce good results.
Virtue is the health, beauty, and well-being of the soul.
When the heart and mind are pure, clean, and healthy,
Then the body will follow suit.
If there is something wrong with the body,
Change the heart before mind gets hold of it.
And then the body will re-suit.
Vice is the disease, weakness, and deformity of the soul.

The Death Poem

I walked upon the earth where Darkness dwells.
I wandered trapped in a foul body on a foul land.
I AM Perfection, hidden from Darkness.
Roaming on this corrupt earth,
On past the imperfect jealous God, of imperfect creation—
Tromping on the Imitator—on past everything I stand.

A master of matter I pass all things.
I AM undressed from the body of Imitation, and all it brings.
Darkness can have its empty carcass—it's deceased.
Darkness can have its empty mass—it's only a disguise.
Everything is an imitation from my homeland.
On past everything, I AM.

A Phantom In The Night

A silhouette,
Thrilling the night!
Awe-inspiring
Bone Chilling dimness.
A phantom in the night!

The Devil

The Devil laid there in the grave!
Struck by lightning – Stood in rage!
Bound in fire he shook his fist!
White hair and fuming eyes –
He looked up and cursed the skies!
His tombstone broke –
He's wrapped in chains!
He's skin and bone – Has rags that hang!
Bolts of lightning, round his head –
He bled on earth – Now he's dead.

The Queen Of The Sea

The Queen of the Sea,
Dressed in her blue cloak of eternity,
She rules the tempestuous sea.
She is the Queen of Peace and Plenty.
She is the Star of the Sea.
She lulls the tempest.
She rules the tempestuous sea –
She is the Goddess of sea farers.
She tames hailstorms, whirlwinds, and lightning.
From the North Seas, to the South Seas,
She is the guardian of sailors and fishermen.
She rules the seas, skies, and infinity.
With her mystical powers over water,
In her element, in the midst of pirates and warships,
She is the armed Goddess of Liberty, Truth, and Justice.

The Queen of the Sea,
On her epic voyage,
Plowing through the heavy seas,
In her hand carved vessel of oak and pine,
As freezing rain and wind howls through her royal ship,
Escorted by dolphins, mermaids, and sea nymphs,
Standing on her ship's bow,
Her pure beauty, a fair virgin in flowing long golden hair,
She bares her breast and calms the raging sea –
In her element, bearing her sextant at the helm,
Guided by the moon and stars,
She navigates through the seas –
She regulates the course of the sun and stars.
She is the guardian of seamen.
She is the Queen of the Sea.

He'll lose his mind
He'll drive like hell

He's pure energy on the line
He has sparks round his mind
He'll drive the peddle through the floor
He'll leave'em all behind

A beast on the track – shattering sound
They'll quake and tremble
He'll lead'em all round
Madness

Round and round
Runny eyes, the wind in his face
His track, the cries
He'll lead the pace

Driving fast, flying free
Soaring round the track with velocity
The power of a beast
A will to win – the greatest speed

A Run-in with the pack
Wild thoughts abound
He won't look back, along the edge
Free again – he'll live or die

Pure energy
Sparks round his mind
Driving the peddle through the floor
He'll leave'em all behind

Come On

Come on grab the hoe.
We'll walk out into the night.
We'll travel through the wilderness.
We'll give it all our might!

We'll dig for plots,
We'll plant them all.
With all the magnificent spots,
We'll be standing mighty tall.

Come on pick your feet up.
In the dark night or moon –
We'll hoof it and never give up!
It'll be light soon.

Illuminating The Way

I live the great mystery.
The unnamed and named.
I act without effort and teach without words.
Happiness is the Way.
Pure and selfless I empty my heart and mind.
I practice not doing.

Hidden and always present,
The Father of things is empty and inexhaustible.
Eliminating judgments I offer my treasures to everyone.
Being centered is empty and inexhaustible.
Sitting quietly,
I find the truth within.

The root of creation is the mysterious feminine.
Listening to her voice she reveals her presence.
It will never end.
Selfless and durable I put myself last.
I live in accordance with nature.
Like water I flow to low ground.

I empty my cup and it becomes full.
I dwell in humility and Love saves me.
I see myself in all and opposites dissolve.
I avoid separation by embracing the one.
I open and close heaven's door by playing the feminine part.
By being with primal virtue I bring heaven to earth.

Being centered in emptiness I make room for what is.
I observe the world and trust my inner vision.
Allowing things to come and go I prefer what is within.
I love myself and everyone.
When I have no self I have no trouble.
I see myself as everything.
Merging as one being invisible, inaudible, and intangible,
Returning to nothingness there is no beginning or end.
In harmony the way things have always been.
From stillness life arises.
Always being empty I keep the way.
Always giving I receive.

All endings are beginnings.
I am totally empty and my heart is at peace.
Returning to the source I find Peace.
Being impartial I am Divine.
Leaving no trace of myself I am the greatest leader.
Because the world has fallen into chaos I appear.

Seeing simplicity I realize my true nature.
I remove selfishness and temper desire.
Being free from care I am being done.
No mind, no worries, I take sustenance from the great Mother.
I see what is within me, the breath of all things.
I follow the great Mother alone.

Being whole I am flexible and bending.
Everything flows to me.
Being one with the way I am one with goodness.
My ways are those of heaven and its power flows through me.
By walking the path I remove superfluous excess.
I come from greatness.

Eternally flowing and returning I am great and boundless.
I understand the great within myself.
Poised and centered I am stable being in touch with my root.
Knowing truth I leave no trace.
Following the light I help all beings impartially.
In humility with my original qualities I govern everything.

In virtue I keep Mother's care.
I know the white and keep the black.
I am one with the infinite.
I act in accord with eternal power.
I am the fountain of the world.
Preserving my original qualities I am unformed.

In humility I achieve greatness.
When I achieve greatness there is no humility.
I do nothing and everything is done.
When there is, no I, I am good.
In humility I am noble.
In lowliness I am exalted.

I gain by losing.
I achieve harmony by combining the yin and embracing yang.
I remain soft and supple and overcome the strong.
I know the value of nonaction.
Love is the fruit of sacrifice.
I give with pure gratitude.

In stillness and tranquility I know myself.
Being content I find the bliss of eternity.
By daily diminishing I find the way.
By giving up learning,
I let things go their own way and achieve mastery.
When doing nothing, nothing is left undone.

Because the nature of my being is kindness,
I am aware of the needs of others.
I see everything as myself.
I love everyone as my own.
I realize my essence.
I am Life.

I honor the Way and value its virtue.
The Way has zero demands.
Spontaneously I worship and give my love to the Father.
The Way gives me Life and Virtue clothes me.
The beginning is my Eternal Mother.
I hold onto my Mother.

I embrace Silence in primal union.
I am free to be myself.
The world governs itself.
I impose nothing.
I am fit to lead because I know no limits.
I am deeply rooted and firmly planted in the Way

I have room for Love because there is no enemy.
The secret to health is to think healthy.
I prefer what is within to what is without.
I am strong by being soft and flexible.
I can give because there is no end to my wealth.
I am like water.

Paradise is wherever I am.
I am in Peace.
I am unattached from everything in the world.
I act for the good of all.
I give my all.
There is no end to my wealth.

Edwards Brothers Malloy
Oxnard, CA USA
March 12, 2015